Low Carb
High Fat Baking

Copyright © 2012 by Mariann Andersson
English Translation copyright © 2013 by Skyhorse Publishing
First published in 2012 as *Baka med LCHF* by Mariann Andersson, Bonnier Fakta, Sweden

Photography by Martin Skredsvik
Author's Assistant and Illustrations by Elisabeth Andersson
Graphic Design by John Losciale

Skyhorse Publishing books may be purchased in bulk at special discounts for sales promotion, corporate gifts, fund-raising, or educational purposes. Special editions can also be created to specifications. For details, contact the Special Sales Department, Skyhorse Publishing, 307 West 36th Street, 11th Floor, New York, NY 10018 or info@skyhorsepublishing.com.

Skyhorse® and Skyhorse Publishing® are registered trademarks of Skyhorse Publishing, Inc.®, a Delaware corporation.

www.skyhorsepublishing.com

10 9 8 7 6 5 4 3 2 1

Library of Congress Cataloging-in-Publication Data is available on file.

ISBN: 978-1-62636-042-6

Printed in China

Low Carb High Fat Baking

Over 40 Gluten- and Sugar-free Pastries, Desserts, and Delicious Treats

Photography by Martin Skredsvik
Translated by Malou Fickling

Mariann Andersson

Skyhorse Publishing

Contents

FOREWORD

I began following a low carbohydrate, high fat lifestyle (LCHF) almost four years ago, and it has made me feel great. Sugar cravings don't bother me anymore—they disappeared as soon as I made the LCHF switch in my diet. While I continued to bake in the usual way for family get-togethers and parties, I made a dessert of berries and cream for myself. However, when my husband and daughter decided to join me in eating LCHF foods, it became necessary to find alternative baked goods to serve at special occasions and weekend coffee klatches.

It's important that my LCHF lifestyle be inclusive and compatible with the rest of my life. Like many people, I have a family, and with family come festivities, along with a variety of occasions to indulge in treats and seasonal goodies. Being able to throw parties and birthday bashes, or just have a few friends over for coffee and a little cake is both lovely and gratifying; this is why I have gathered a collection of delicious LCHF recipes to share with you in this book.

An early encounter with LCHF baking occurred when I placed my first order for coconut flour from a low-carb specialty store in January 2011, as I was planning to use it in a coconut cake instead of coconut flakes. As soon as the flour arrived, I set about baking the cake, and used the same amount of coconut flour as the recommended amount of ground coconut flakes in the original recipe.

I thought the batter would end up runny as usual, but instead found myself dealing with an enormous lump of dough. Well, I decided to go ahead and bake the dough anyway: I spread it out on a small, oblong sheet pan and placed it in the oven. Once the baking time was up

and I pulled the dough out of the oven, what a surprise—it had turned into a piecrust! I realized that if you press the dough in a pie dish and thin it out along the edges, the end result is a piecrust that looks and tastes absolutely identical to a traditional crust made with wheat flour.

Following this discovery, I combed through books and websites searching for Swedish recipes containing coconut flour, but came up empty. However, I did find a smattering of American recipes which I have subsequently used as a base for my culinary experiments and all my recipes.

I hope that this book will inspire you to bake with LCHF, and above all, I wish to show you that you don't have to abstain from eating festive holiday-themed foods with family and friends in order to follow the LCHF way successfully. Imagine once again being able to properly celebrate Fat Tuesday, Waffle Day, or even indulge in a slice of pancake cake that you have baked with your kids! These occasions are the sweetest celebrations of life.

Enjoy!

Mariann

BAKING LOW CARB HIGH FAT

INSTEAD OF FLOUR

Coconut flour is one of the main, basic ingredients I use in LCHF baking, as it is both dense—so a little goes a long way—and, more important, contains few carbohydrates—on an average 3 grams carbohydrates per 14 grams of flour. When a cake calls for 1–1¼ cup of wheat flour you may only need to use ¼ to ½ cup of coconut flour.

Coconut flour differs slightly from other nut flours traditionally used in LCHF baking. In appearance and texture it is similar to all-purpose flour, yet it exhibits none of all-purpose flour's downsides. Notably, baked goods with coconut flour as a base don't require long baking times, making them a quick treat to fix and serve, and perhaps also more environmentally friendly. Also, pastries made with coconut flour (and other LCHF flours) are suitable for diabetics, people suffering from gluten-intolerance, or those simply following a low-carbohydrate diet. If you are lactose intolerant, recipes made with LCHF flours can easily be adapted: simply substitute the dairy ingredients with lactose-free alternatives, such as nut milks or gluten-free oat milk.

Please be aware that coconut flour is not the same as ground coconut flakes, and that you cannot turn coconut flakes into flour by grinding them in a food processor. Ignoring this directive will doom your recipe to fail, and your dessert might more closely resemble an omelet than a cake. Coconut flour has a high fiber content (61%) and is a byproduct of coconut milk production. In its raw state it has a slightly sweet aroma and a faint taste of coconut, but it will not add a coconut flavor to your baked goods. If you are seeking a coconut flavor you must add coconut flakes to your recipe.

A convenient flour to use is Bob's Red Mill Coconut Flour as it can be found in the baking section of larger grocery chains. You can also find several brands online, and check out your local co-op food store's bulk bins.

INSTEAD OF SUGAR

With regards to sweeteners in LCHF baking, simply replace sugar with LCHF-approved sweeteners such as erythritol and Stevia.

Zerose, Organic Zero, and Zsweet are some sugar-substitutes marketed under different names. They all consist of erythritol, a sugar alcohol that is naturally found in pears and melons, among other fruits. Erythritol is produced industrially from glucose through the process of fermentation, and thus this sweetener can be found in all foodstuffs that ferment. Stevia is a sugar-substitute extracted from the plant *Stevia rebaudiana*.

My family tends to suffer from sore throats from high doses of erythritol in baked goods, while others find that it calls up an assertively strong metallic taste; I find the best-tasting sweetness comes from a combination of erythritol and Stevia.

To mix the two sweeteners, I recommend using powdered erythritol, which is the Organic Zero equivalent to confectioners' sugar. You can make erythritol powder at home by grinding erythritol in a food processor into flour; however, it is likely that the store-bought powder will be much more finely ground than the homemade version, and thus will impart a significantly less metallic aftertaste.

Stevia is intensely sweet, and it can therefore be challenging to get the right dose for baking. It's available in various strengths, so it follows that the higher the strength, the less of it you will need in your dessert. The recipes in this book call for erythritol powder along with a grade of Stevia that is two hundred times sweeter than sugar, so the general rule of thumb is that for every 3 tablespoons Organic Zero, add a maximum of ⅛ tsp Stevia (although feel free to increase the amount of Stevia if you prefer a sweeter pastry). If you already know that erythritol doesn't leave you with an unpleasant aftertaste, you can exclude the Stevia altogether in favor of Organic Zero.

Please note that many cakes baked with regular sugar develop a rich crust that cannot be replicated with sugar substitutes such as Zsweet or Stevia. Also, regular sugar has a preservative and moisturizing effect that Zsweet and Stevia lack, so low-carbohydrate pastries tend to not have as long shelf-life as regular treats. Consequently, LCHF baked goods should be enjoyed the same day they are baked, or the next day at the latest. Happily, most LCHF goods are suitable for freezing.

Low carb pastries, by their very nature, do not taste as sweet as their traditionally sugared counterparts because the doses of sugar substitutes are deliberately kept low. Since people on low-carbohydrate diets are used to less sugar, they do not have as strong a hankering for sweetened foods, so take care not to overdo it on the sweeteners.

It is also essential to keep in mind that because there is less intensity in the sweetening of the food, the recipes in the book call exclusively for unsalted butter. Many believe that salt enhances flavor, and while this is true in traditional recipes where the salt counterbalances and enhances the sugar, in LCHF baking salt can quickly overwhelm the other, more subtle, flavors, and thus should be used very sparingly.

Those who still have a strong sweet tooth might find the flavor of these pastries to be

fairly muted, whereas those who are more accustomed to low-carbohydrate foods will find that it suits their palates better as it allows the flavor of chocolate or other spices to emerge more distinctly.

I also want to point out that for special occasions, you can choose to add a little sugar to the dessert by incorporating high-quality chocolate with a high cocoa content. If you'd rather not use sugar at all, it can be replaced with raw chocolate or cocoa powder. The cake will taste different and you will need to adjust the seasonings by adding a little more sweetener to the ingredients.

There is an ongoing debate on the topic of sweeteners and synthesized sugar substitutes, particularly aspartame and sucralose. The LCHF-approved sweeteners used in low-carbohydrate baking are completely natural and don't cause side effects, and therefore will have no effect on your blood sugar level.

This in turn may reduce your cravings for sweet foods—as well as keeping you full and satisfied for hours—as you will not be at the mercy of your surging and plummeting blood sugar, which creates the cravings in the first place!

CAN LOW CARBOHYDRATE PASTRIES BE CONSIDERED FOOD?

Let's take a look at the nutritional profile of a Mocha Cake (page 86):

    Carbohydrates: 14 grams, or 3%
    Protein: 61 grams, or 12%
    Fat: 425 grams, or 85%

According to LCHF, a good nutritional balance can be found in foods that are made up of a maximum of 5% carbohydrates, 15–20% protein, and the remainder in fat. This makes the Mocha Cake a good fit for the LCHF diet,

despite containing slightly too little protein and a bit more fat. What is essential to take into account here is that the carbohydrate content of this cake is far lower than the recommended amount, which is after all the main objective of low-carbohydrate nutrition. (Furthermore, if the ideal balance cannot be achieved it is preferable to err on the side of eating less protein and more fat than the other way around.)

The recipes throughout this book follow these general guidelines, increasing in carbohydrate count only if served with excess cream and berries. If you choose to omit those extra garnishes, all the baked goods can be considered "food" rather than "treats," as one could easily enjoy a pastry instead of, say, lunch, skipping the more traditional meal in good conscience and feeling full and satisfied to boot. After all, these pastries are made primarily from

eggs and butter, which are both healthy and LCHF approved ingredients!

A final note about these recipes: the number of portions that each item serves applies if you are baking one single type of pastry—a big cake for a birthday party, for example. On the other hand, if you are planning on making a wider variety of goods to include in a buffet, these cakes and pastries will serve more people than suggested by each recipe.

Happy baking!

WHAT SHOULD I HAVE IN MY PANTRY AND REFRIGERATOR?

To bake LCHF goods you will need to add new basic ingredients to your pantry in order to replace traditional sugar and plain flour. Many of these items can be bought at grocery stores, food co-ops, and online (a list of websites is provided on page 94). Other ingredients widely used in LCHF baking include staples that are familiar and found in most household refrigerators and pantries. See below for an index of recurring ingredients, as well as definitions and uses for lesser-known, more LCHF-specific items.

Sweeteners:

OrganicZero: erythritol, a sugar alcohol (naturally occurring in fruits)

Zsweet: erythritol and *Stevia rebaudiana*

Stevia: extracted from the plant *Stevia rebaudiana*.

Flours:

Coconut flour: a byproduct of coconut milk production.

Almond flour and hazelnut flour: can be purchased ready-made, or made at home by grinding whole nuts into flour in an almond, coffee or Magic Bullet-type grinder.

Psyllium Husk: sold as Whole Psyllium Husks and Psyllium Powder. Bulking agent. Mixed with liquids, psyllium husk expands and forms a gelatinous mass. Some might experience a gritty feel when chewing it, so we generally limit its use to one tablespoon per recipe.

NutraFiber: a fiber from beet pulp. Bulking agent. NutraFiber retains 4 to 5 times its own weight in fluid. Dosage about 3 tablespoons per recipe. Ground NutraFiber is useful for coating baking pans.

Pantry Staples:

Unsweetened coconut flakes and coconut chips. Cocoa powder*, cocoa nibs and raw chocolate, or high-quality dark chocolate with a cocoa content of at least 70%. Almonds, bitter almonds, and a variety of nuts. Vanilla beans, unsweetened vanilla powder (ground vanilla bean), or pure vanilla extract. Baking powder and baking soda.

Refrigerated Staples:

Large eggs, unsalted butter, and full-fat cream cheese. Whipping cream, crème fraîche, and full-fat sour cream.

Useful Ingredients:

Unflavored Gelatin: leaf or powder. Cream of Tartar. Limes, lemons, passion fruits, a selection of unsweetened frozen and fresh berries.

*There are two types of cocoa powder: Dutch-processed and natural unsweetened.

Dutch-processed cocoa is mild, its acids neutralized. Must be used with baking powder unless acidic ingredients are added.

Natural unsweetened cocoa is bitter and gives a deep chocolate flavor.

COOKIES AND BITES

Chocolate Pinwheels

SERVES 10–14

Ingredients:

Dough
7 tbsp (100 g) unsalted butter, softened
2 tbsp erythritol powder and ¹⁄₁₆ tsp stevia powder
3 large eggs + 1 egg yolk
¾ cup (200 ml) coconut flour
½ tsp vanilla powder or 1 tsp pure vanilla extract

Filling
⅓ cup (75 g) unsalted butter
2 tbsp erythritol powder and ¹⁄₁₆ tsp stevia powder
⅔ cup (150 ml) almond flour
3 tbsp cocoa powder
½ tsp vanilla powder or 1 tsp pure vanilla extract

Garnish
1 egg white, lightly beaten
chopped hazelnuts

METHOD:

Preheat oven to 300–350°F (150–175°C). Line a cookie sheet with parchment paper.

Dough
In a food processor cream butter and sweetener. Add eggs, one at a time, beating well between additions, scraping down the sides if needed. Add the extra egg yolk and continue mixing until light and airy. If using vanilla extract, add this now.

Mix coconut flour and—if using—vanilla powder. Add dry mix to the batter working until you have a smooth dough.

Between two sheets of parchment paper roll out the dough to a thickness of about ¼ inch (½ cm) keeping the dough as rectangular as possible.

Filling
Melt butter with sweetener. Stir vigorously, making sure that the sweetener dissolves completely. If using vanilla extract, add this now. Incorporate almond flour, cocoa powder, and—if using—vanilla powder. Let cool.

Spread filling on top of dough and make a compact roll. Refrigerate roll for 30 minutes.

With a sharp knife cut roll into 10 slices, roughly ½ inch (1 cm) thick. Place slices on the prepared cookie sheet. Can be placed close together as these cookies won't spread.

Brush with lightly whipped egg white and sprinkle with chopped hazelnuts.

Bake in center of oven at 300–350°F (150–175°C) for 10 to 15 minutes. Ovens do vary so start checking at the earlier time. Cool on wire rack.

➤ TIP: **For nut allergies**: exchange the filling's almond flour with ½ cup (100 ml) ground NutraFiber. Ground flour-like NutraFiber will also reduce the cookie's carbohydrate content. Replace hazelnut garnish with coconut flakes.

Cinnamon Pinwheels

SERVES 10–14

Ingredients:

Dough
7 tbsp (100 g) soft unsalted butter
2 tbsp erythritol powder and ¹⁄₁₆ tsp
   stevia powder
3 large eggs + 1 egg yolk
¾ cup (200 ml) coconut flour
1 tsp ground cardamom

Filling
⅓ cup (75 g) unsalted butter
2 tbsp erythritol powder and ¹⁄₁₆ tsp
   stevia powder
⅔ cup (150 ml) almond flour
2 tbsp cinnamon

Garnish
1 egg white, whipped
chopped almonds

METHOD:

Preheat the oven to 300–350°F (150–175°C). Line a cookie sheet with parchment paper.

Dough
Cream butter and sweetener. Add eggs and additional egg yolk, one at a time, beating well between each addition. Continue beating until pale and airy.

Blend coconut flour and cardamom, then add it to batter. Work all ingredients into a smooth dough.

Roll dough between two sheets of parchment paper to a thickness of about ¼ inch (½ cm) making it as rectangular as possible.

Filling
Melt butter with sweetener, stirring until the sweetener dissolves completely. Work in almond flour and cinnamon. Let cool.

Spread cinnamon filling on top of dough and roll dough into a compact roll. Refrigerate for 30 minutes.

With a sharp knife cut roll into 10 slices, roughly ½ inch (1 cm) thick. Place the slices on the prepared cookie sheet. These cookies won't spread, so they can be placed close together. Brush with lightly whipped egg white and sprinkle with chopped almonds.

Bake on center rack at 300–350°F (150–175°C) for 10 to 15 minutes. Ovens do vary so start checking at the earlier time. Cool on a wire rack.

➤ **TIP: For nut allergies:** replace almond flour with ½ cup (100 ml) ground NutraFiber. Ground flour-like NutraFiber will also reduce the cookies' carbohydrate content. Replace almond garnish with coconut flakes.

Lime Swirls

SERVES 10–14

Ingredients:

Dough
7 tbsp (100 g) soft unsalted butter
2 tbsp erythritol powder and
  ¹⁄₁₆ tsp stevia powder
3 large eggs + 1 egg yolk
the juice of 2 limes—grate zest to
  use in filling
½ tsp vanilla powder or 1 tsp pure
  vanilla extract
¾ cup (200 ml) coconut flour

Filling
⅓ cup (75 g) unsalted butter
2 tbsp erythritol powder and
  ¹⁄₁₆ tsp stevia powder
⅔ cup (150 ml) almond flour

Garnish
1 whipped egg white
grated coconut flakes

METHOD:

Preheat oven to 300–350°F (150–175°C). Line a cookie sheet with parchment paper. Grate lime zest for filling.

Dough
Cream butter and sweetener. Add the eggs one at a time, beating well between each addition. Add the extra yolk and beat until light and airy. Add in lime juice. If using vanilla extract, add this now.

Mix vanilla powder—if using—with coconut flour and add it to the batter. Work it into a smooth dough.

Roll dough between two sheets of parchment paper to a thickness of about ¼ inch (½ cm), making it as rectangular as possible.

Filling
Melt butter with sweetener, stirring until the sweetener has completely dissolved. Add almond flour and lime zest. Let cool.

Spread lime filling on top of dough, and roll the dough into a compact roll. Refrigerate for 30 minutes.

With a sharp knife cut the roll into 10 slices, roughly ½ inch (1 cm) thick. Place them on the prepared cookie sheet. These cookies won't spread, so no need for careful spacing. Brush with whipped egg white and sprinkle with coconut flakes.

Bake on center rack at 300–350°F (150–175°C) for 10 to 15 minutes. Ovens do vary so start checking at the earlier time. Cool on wire rack.

TIP: For nut allergies: replace the almond flour with ½ cup (100 ml) ground NutraFiber. Ground flour-like NutraFiber will also reduce the cookies' carbohydrate content.

For that touch of luxury, add a dash of rum to the filling!

Almond Bites

SERVES 10–12

Ingredients:

7 tbsp (100 g) soft unsalted butter
2 tbsp erythritol powder and $\frac{1}{16}$ tsp stevia powder
3 large eggs + 1 egg yolk
$\frac{1}{3}$ cup (100 ml) almonds
3–4 bitter almonds or 1 tsp almond extract
$\frac{1}{2}$ cup (100 ml) almond flour

Garnish

1 egg white, whipped
slivered almonds

METHOD:

Blanch and peel the almonds. Grate lime zest and juice limes. Preheat the oven to 350°F (175°C). Line a cookie sheet with parchment paper.

Cream butter and sweetener. Add eggs, one at a time, beating well between each addition. Follow with the extra egg yolk, beating until pale and airy.

Pulse almonds and bitter almonds in a coffee or Magic Bullet-type grinder.

Add ground almonds and coconut flour to the batter. Combine all ingredients and work to a smooth dough. Refrigerate for 30 minutes.

With a sharp knife, cut the dough into 10 to 12 pieces and form plump rectangular cookies. Place cookies on the prepared cookie sheet. Brush with lightly whipped egg white and sprinkle with slivered almonds. Bake on center rack at 350°F (175°C) for about 15 minutes. Cool on wire rack.

◆▶ **TIP:** Remove the almond skin easily by rubbing the wet almonds between two kitchen towels. Dry thoroughly before grinding.

Almond Tarts with Lime Cream

10 TARTS

Ingredients:

Tart Shells

⅓ cup (75 g) unsalted butter, very
    soft
1 tbsp erythritol powder and
    ¹⁄₁₆ tsp stevia powder
1 large egg
½ (100 ml) almond flour
¼ cup (50 ml) coconut flour

Lime Cream

2 limes, zest and juice
2 large eggs
2 tbsp erythritol powder and
    ⅛ tsp stevia powder
⅓ cup (75 g) unsalted butter, very
    soft

Garnish

strawberries
grated lime peel (optional)

METHOD:

Preheat oven to 350°F (175°C). Grate and juice limes.

Tart Shells

Cream butter and sweetener. Whisk in the egg. Mix almond flour and coconut flour, pressing out any lumps, and add to batter.

Press dough into 10 individual round tartlet tins. Bake at 350°F (175°C) for about 10 minutes. Allow to cool.

Lime Cream

In a saucepan, combine eggs, sweetener, lime zest, and juice and bring to a simmer. Simmer until cream thickens some. *Do not boil!*

Remove pan from heat and strain cream into a bowl. With the aid of a stainless steel strainer and a spoon, push the cream through with a back and forth motion. Cool cream to room temperature.

Incorporate the very soft butter, a little bit at a time.

When tart shells have cooled completely, fill with lime cream and garnish with sliced strawberries and grated lime peel.

◆➤ **TIP:** Shells can be frozen—simply omit the filling. Limes may be replaced with lemons.

The shells are equally delicious filled with whipped cream and berries.

Mazarin Tarts

SERVES 12

Ingredients:

Shells

½ cup (125 g) unsalted butter
2 large eggs
3 tbsp erythritol powder and ⅟₁₆ tsp
    stevia powder
⅔ cup (150 ml) coconut flour
1½ tsp baking powder
½ tsp vanilla powder or 1 tsp pure
    vanilla extract

Filling

⅔ cup (200 ml) almonds
1 to 2 bitter almonds or 1 tsp
    almond extract—optional
3 tbsp erythritol powder and ⅛ tsp
    stevia powder
2 tbsp whipping cream
⅓ cup (75 g) unsalted butter,
    softened
3 large eggs

METHOD:

Preheat oven to 350°F (175°C). Blanch almonds and remove skins. Dry thoroughly. Melt butter and cool.

Shells

Beat eggs and sweetener until light and airy. Add the melted and cooled butter to the egg mixture. If using vanilla extract, add this now.

Combine coconut flour with baking powder and—if using—vanilla powder. Work mixture into the batter to make a dough. Press dough into individual mazarin tins while making sure that dough covers the edges. Keep the dough's thickness to about ¼ inch (½ cm).

Filling

Grind almonds in a nut grinder, or pulse them in a coffee or Magic Bullet-type grinder. In a food processor mix ground almonds with the erythritol/stevia mix. Continue mixing 5 minutes. Add cream, a little at a time, until desired consistency. Cut butter into smaller pieces and work it into almond paste to make a smooth dough. Add the eggs, one at a time.

Spoon filling into the pastry lined mazarin tins. Bake at 350°F (175°C) for about 15 minutes. The tarts are ready when filling is firm. Cool on wire rack.

To serve, dust with powdered erythritol.

◆→ **TIP:** For convenience, make a larger batch of almond paste. Freeze portions in tin foil and just defrost to use. Preferably grate the almond paste before mixing it with the other ingredients.

Raspberry Thumb Print Cookies

SERVES 16

Ingredients:

7 tbsp (100 g) unsalted butter, softened

3 tbsp erythritol powder and ⅛ tsp stevia powder

3 large eggs

¾ cup (200 ml) coconut flour

1 tsp vanilla powder or 1 tsp pure vanilla extract

16 raspberries

METHOD:

Preheat oven to 350°F (175°C). Line a cookie sheet with parchment paper.

Cream butter and sweetener. Add eggs, one at a time and whisk until light and airy. Add vanilla extract, if using.

Mix coconut flour and—if using—vanilla powder and add it to the batter. Mix into a smooth dough. Refrigerate dough for about 30 minutes.

Make 16 ball-shaped cookies. The dough will not spread, so place cookies fairly close together on the prepared baking sheet. With your thumb, make an indent deep enough to hold a raspberry in the dough balls. Place raspberry in center and bake in the middle of the oven at 350°F (175°C) for 10 to 15 minutes. Cool on wire rack.

COFFEE CAKES, BROWNIES, AND BUNS

Brownies

SERVES 12

Ingredients:

3½ oz (100 g) cream cheese
½ tsp vanilla powder or 1 tsp pure
 vanilla extract
5 tbsp cocoa powder
3 tbsp erythritol powder and
 ⅛ tsp stevia powder
⅔ cup (150 g) unsalted butter,
 softened
½ cup (100 ml) whipping cream
5 large eggs
⅔ cup (150 ml) coconut flour
1 tsp baking powder
⅔ cup (150 ml) chopped walnuts
 or pecans (optional)

METHOD:

Preheat oven to 350°F (175°C). Line a 6 x 9 inch (15 x 23 cm) brownie pan with parchment paper. Coarsely chop nuts.

In a stand mixer beat cream cheese, vanilla powder/extract, cocoa, and sweetener until smooth. Add the softened butter a little at a time. Add the cream then the eggs, one at a time, mixing well between additions, until smooth.

Blend coconut flour and baking powder. Mix thoroughly into the batter, pressing out any lumps. Add chopped nuts if using.

Spoon the batter into the prepared pan and bake at 350°F (175°C) for 10 to 15 minutes. Watch carefully: the center—about 1 inch (3 cm) in from the edge—should still be wobbly. Remove from oven and let cool in pan on wire rack.

Wrap the cake—still in its pan—in plastic wrap or a plastic bag. Refrigerate overnight.

Note: DO NOT skip the refrigeration!

To serve, cut cooled cake into portions.

◆▶**TIP:** Freeze cake in portions, layering with plastic wrap or tin foil.

Chocolate and Mazarin Cake

SERVES 12–14

Ingredients:

Mazarin Layer

1⅓ cups (200 g) almonds + 3 bitter
  almonds (optional)
3 tbsp erythritol powder and ⅛ tsp
  stevia powder
3–4 tbsp whipping cream
⅔ cup (150 g) unsalted butter
3 large eggs
3 tbsp coconut flour

Chocolate Layer

⅔ cup (150 g) unsalted butter,
  melted and cooled
3 tbsp erythritol powder and ¹⁄₁₆ tsp
  stevia powder
4 large eggs
½ cup (100 ml) whipping cream
⅔ cup (150 ml) coconut flour
6 tbsp cocoa powder
½ tsp vanilla powder or 1 tsp pure
  vanilla extract
unsweetened cocoa nibs

METHOD:

Blanch and skin almonds. Grind almonds using an almond grinder, or pulse in a coffee or Magic Bullet-type grinder. Preheat oven to 350°F (175°C).

Mazarin Layer

Place ground almonds and sweetener in a food processor and pulse a few minutes. Add cream, one tablespoon at a time, until the almond paste reaches suitable consistency.

Leave almond paste in food processor; pulse in butter. Add eggs, one at a time, and pulse until smooth. Put almond paste in bowl and stir in flour by hand.

Spread batter over bottom of a 8–9 inch (21–24 cm) springform pan. Make sure that the batter covers the edges.

Chocolate Layer

Beat eggs and sweetener a few minutes until light and airy. Add cream and melted and cooled butter. If using vanilla extract, add this now.

In a bowl mix coconut flour with cocoa powder and—if using—vanilla powder. Stir dry ingredients into batter and mix thoroughly until smooth.

Spread chocolate mixture over mazarin batter and sprinkle with cocoa nibs. Bake at 350°F (175°C) for 20 minutes.

◆▶**TIP:** Eat the cake "as is"; it will practically melt in your mouth just like a chocolate truffle. Or, add a dollop of whipped cream and some berries.

Note that this cake does not spread. Take care to cover the edges evenly with the batter and remember to neaten the top layer.

Chocolate Swiss Roll

SERVES 10–14

Ingredients:

Cake Layer
4 large eggs
3 tbsp erythritol powder and ⅛ tsp
   stevia powder
½ cup (100 ml) coconut flour
1 tbsp psyllium husk
1½ tsp baking powder

Butter Cream
3½ oz (100 g) full fat cream cheese
4 tbsp cocoa powder
2 tbsp erythritol powder and ¹⁄₁₆ tsp
   stevia powder
½ tsp vanilla powder or 1 tsp pure
   vanilla extract
⅓ cup (75 g) unsalted butter,
   softened
whipping cream (optional)

METHOD:

*Preheat oven to 350°F (175°C). Line an 8 x 12 inch
(20 x 30 cm) rimmed baking sheet with parchment paper.*

Cake Layer
Beat eggs and sweetener until light and airy. Mix coconut flour, psyllium husk and baking powder. Stir dry ingredients thoroughly into egg mixture, leaving no lumps.

Spread batter on the prepared baking sheet. Bake at 350°F (175°C) for 5 to 8 minutes. Cake is ready when dry to the touch.

Turn cake onto a clean piece of parchment paper. Cool cake on wire rack.

Butter Cream
Mix cream cheese, cocoa powder, sweetener and vanilla until smooth. Stir in butter in small batches. Add the (optional) cream until mixture is of a buttery and spreadable consistency.

Spread butter cream over cake layer and roll it up Swiss Roll-fashion. Keep refrigerated.

Slice before serving.

Dreamy Swiss Roll

SERVES 10–14

Ingredients:

Cake Layer
4 large eggs
3 tbsp erythritol powder and ¹⁄₁₆ tsp
    stevia powder
½ cup (100 ml) coconut flour
1 tbsp psyllium husk
4 tbsp cocoa powder
1½ tsp baking powder

Butter Cream
⅔ cup (150 g) unsalted butter, very soft
½ tsp vanilla powder or 1 tsp pure vanilla
    extract
1¾ oz (50 g) cream cheese
2 tbsp erythritol powder and ¹⁄₁₆ tsp
    stevia powder
whipping cream (optional)

METHOD:

Preheat oven to 350°F (175°C). Line an 8 x 12 inch
(20 x 30 cm) rimmed baking sheet with parchment paper.

Cake Layer
Beat eggs and sweetener until light and airy. Mix coconut flour psyllium husk, cocoa powder, and baking powder. Stir dry ingredients thoroughly into egg mixture, leaving no lumps.

Spread batter onto the prepared baking sheet. Bake at 350°F (175°C) for 5 to 8 minutes. Cake is ready when dry to the touch.

Turn the cake onto a clean piece of parchment paper. Cool on wire rack.

Butter Cream
Blend ingredients until smooth. Add some cream for softer consistency.

Cover cake layer with butter cream and roll it up Swiss Roll-fashion. Refrigerate.

Slice before serving.

Lime Swiss Roll

SERVES 10–14

Ingredients:

Cake Layer
4 large eggs
3 tbsp erythritol powder and ¹⁄₁₆ tsp
    stevia powder
½ cup (100 ml) coconut flour
1½ tbsp psyllium husk
2 tbsp cocoa powder
1½ tsp baking powder
1 tbsp lime juice (about 2 limes)

Lime Cream
⅔ cup (150 g) unsalted butter, softened
1¾ oz (50 g) cream cheese
1 large egg yolk
zest from 2 limes
3 tbsp erythritol powder and ¹⁄₁₆ tsp stevia powder

METHOD:

Preheat oven to 350°F (175°C). Zest 2 limes and juice the limes.
   Line an 8 x 12 inch (20 x 30 cm) rimmed baking sheet with parchment paper.

Cake Layer

Beat eggs and sweetener until light and airy. Add lime juice. Mix coconut flour, psyllium husk, cocoa powder, and baking powder. Stir dry ingredients thoroughly into egg mixture, leaving no lumps.
   Spread batter onto prepared baking sheet. Bake at 350°F (175°C) for 5 to 8 minutes. Cake is ready when dry to the touch.
   Turn the cake onto a clean piece of parchment paper. Cool cake layer on wire rack.

Lime Cream

Blend ingredients for the lime cream thoroughly.
   Cover cake layer with lime cream and roll up Swiss Roll-fashion. Refrigerate.
   Slice before serving.

Mocha Swiss Roll

SERVES 10–14

Ingredients:

Cake Layer
4 large eggs
3 tbsp erythritol powder and
   ⅛ tsp stevia powder
½ cup (100 ml) coconut flour
1 tbsp psyllium husk
1½ tsp baking powder

Mocha Cream
7 tbsp (100 g) unsalted butter,
   softened
1¾ oz (50 g) cream cheese
1 tbsp instant coffee dissolved in
   1 tbsp warm water
2 tsp cocoa powder
2 tbsp erythritol powder and
   ¹⁄₁₆ tsp stevia powder
whipping cream (optional)

METHOD:

*Preheat oven to 350°F (175°C). Line an 8 x 12 inch
(20 x 30 cm) rimmed baking sheet with parchment paper.*

Cake Layer

Beat eggs and sweetener until light and airy. In a bowl, mix coconut flour, psyllium husk and baking powder. Mix dry ingredients thoroughly into egg batter, leaving no lumps.
   Spread batter onto the prepared baking sheet. Bake at 350°F (175°C) for 5 to 8 minutes. The cake is ready when dry to the touch.
   Turn cake onto a clean piece of parchment paper. Let cake layer cool on wire rack.

Mocha Cream

Blend ingredients for the mocha cream thoroughly. Add some cream for softer consistency.
   Cover the cake layer with mocha cream, and roll it up Swiss Roll-fashion. Refrigerate. Slice before serving.

Lemon Cake

SERVES 14

Ingredients:

5 large eggs
3 tbsp erythritol powder and
    ⅛ tsp stevia powder
⅔ cup (150 g) unsalted butter,
    melted and cooled
1 cup (200 ml) whipping cream
1 lemon, juice and grated zest
½ cup (100 ml) coconut flour
½ cup (100 ml) almond flour
1½ tbsp psyllium husk
2 tsp baking powder

METHOD:

Preheat oven to 350°F (175°C). Line a 6 cup (1 ½ liter) loaf tin with parchment paper. Melt butter.

Beat eggs and sweetener until light and airy. Add cooled butter and cream to egg batter and whisk.

Add lemon juice and grated zest.

In a bowl, mix dry ingredients and add to batter, leaving no lumps. Spoon batter into prepared loaf tin. Bake at 350°F (175°C) for 35 minutes. The cake is ready when a toothpick inserted in the middle comes out clean.

◆➤**TIP: For nut allergies,** exchange almond flour for 3 tbsp coconut flour.

Cinnamon and Cardamom Coffee Cake

SERVES 14

Ingredients:

Cake
7 tbsp (100 g) unsalted butter,
    melted, cooled
4 large eggs
3 tbsp erythritol powder and
    $\frac{1}{16}$ tsp stevia powder
½ cup (100 ml) whipping cream
½ cup (100 ml) coconut flour
½ cup (100 ml) almond flour
1 tbsp psyllium husks
1 tbsp ground cardamom
2 tsp baking powder

Filling
¼ cup (50 g) unsalted butter
½ cup (100 ml) almond flour
1 tbsp cinnamon
2 tbsp erythritol powder and
    $\frac{1}{16}$ tsp stevia powder

Garnish
slivered almonds

METHOD:

Preheat oven to 350°F (175°C). Line a 6 cup (1 ½ liter) loaf pan with parchment paper. Melt and cool butter.

Cake
Beat eggs and sweetener until light and airy. Whisk cooled butter and cream into the egg mixture.

In a separate bowl, mix dry ingredients then add to batter while stirring, leaving no lumps.

Filling
In a saucepan melt butter, then incorporate remaining ingredients, while mixing thoroughly.

Spoon half of cake batter into prepared pan and layer cinnamon filling on top. Cover with remaining batter. Sprinkle evenly with slivered almonds, lightly pressing them into the surface. Bake at 350°F (175°C) for 30 minutes. The cake is ready when a toothpick inserted in the center comes out dry.

Chocolate Lava Cake

SERVES 8

Ingredients:

⅔ cup (150 g) unsalted butter
½ cup (100 ml) whipping cream
4 large eggs
4 tbsp erythritol powder and ⅛ tsp
    stevia powder
⅓ cup (75 ml) coconut flour
4 tbsp cocoa powder
½ tsp vanilla powder or 1 tsp pure
    vanilla extract

To serve

lightly whipped cream

METHOD:

Preheat oven to 350°F (175°C). Grease and lightly dust an 8 inch (21 cm) springform pan with coconut flour.

In a medium-sized saucepan melt butter. Remove from heat. Stir in cream and sweetener followed by the eggs, one at a time, blending thoroughly after each addition. If using vanilla extract, add this now.

In a separate bowl mix coconut flour, cocoa powder, and if using, vanilla powder. Add to saucepan, mixing thoroughly.

Pour batter into prepared springform pan and bake at 350°F (175°C) for 5 to 10 minutes. Watch carefully—the center of the cake (about 1 inch [3 cm] in) should still be slightly runny. Let cool in pan on wire rack. Serve with lightly whipped cream.

TIP: If you let the cake bake for 10 to 15 minutes, you'll have a most delicious dense chocolate cake.

Sweetheart Squares

SERVES 12

Ingredients:

Cake
6 large eggs
3 tbsp erythritol powder and
    1/16 tsp stevia powder
2/3 cup (150 g) unsalted butter,
    melted and cooled
4 tbsp cocoa powder
1/3 cup (75 ml) coconut flour
1/2 cup (100 ml) almond flour
1/2 tsp vanilla powder or 1 tsp pure
    vanilla extract
2 tsp baking powder

Chocolate Frosting
1 tbsp instant coffee (optional)
7 tbsp (100 g) very soft unsalted
    butter
1¾ oz (50 g) cream cheese
3 tbsp erythritol powder and
    1/16 tsp stevia powder
4 tbsp cocoa powder

Garnish
unsweetened coconut flakes

METHOD:

Preheat oven to 350°F (175°C). Grease and lightly dust a 6 x 9 inch (15 x 23 cm) brownie pan with coconut flour. Melt and cool butter.

Cake
In a bowl, beat eggs and sweetener until light and airy. Whisk the cooled butter into the egg mixture.

    In a separate bowl mix dry ingredients and add to the batter, mixing thoroughly.

    Spoon batter into prepared brownie pan. Bake at 350°F (175°C) for about 20 minutes. The cake is ready when a toothpick inserted in the center comes out clean. Cool on wire rack.

Chocolate Frosting
Dissolve the instant coffee in a little warm water. Combine all frosting ingredients and blend well.

    Spread frosting on cake and garnish with coconut flakes. Keep refrigerated.

    To serve, cut into squares.

➤**TIP:** For a creamier frosting, use 3½ tbsp (50 g) butter and 3½ oz (100 g) cream cheese.
For nut allergies: exchange almond flour for 3 tbsp coconut flour.

Gingerbread Cake

SERVES 14

Ingredients:

5 large eggs
3 tbsp erythritol powder and ⅛ tsp
   stevia powder
⅔ cup (150 g) unsalted butter,
   melted
1 cup (200 ml) whipping cream
½ cup (100 ml) coconut flour
½ cup (100 ml) almond flour
2 tsp baking powder
1 tbsp gingerbread spices

METHOD:

Preheat oven to 350°F (175°C). Line a 6 cup (1 ½ liter) loaf pan with parchment paper. Melt and cool butter.

In a bowl beat eggs and sweetener until light and airy. Add cream and melted butter to egg mixture.

In a separate bowl, mix dry ingredients and incorporate them thoroughly into the batter.

Pour batter into the prepared pan. Bake at 350°F (175°C) for about 35 minutes. The cake is done when a toothpick inserted in the center of the cake comes out clean.

TIP: For a taste "kick," add ¼ cup (50 ml) cranberries and, if needed, some additional sweetener.

For nut allergies: Exchange almond flour for 3 tbsp coconut flour.

Silvia's Cake

Ingredients:

Cake
5 large eggs + 1 egg white
2 tbsp erythritol powder and
  $\frac{1}{16}$ tsp stevia powder
1 cup (250 ml) water
$\frac{2}{3}$ cup (150 ml) coconut flour
2 tsp baking powder
½ tsp vanilla powder or 1 tsp pure
  vanilla extract

Frosting
7 tbsp (100 g) unsalted butter
2 tbsp erythritol powder and
  $\frac{1}{16}$ tsp stevia powder
1 egg yolk
coconut flakes

METHOD:

*Preheat oven to 350°F (175°C). Butter and lightly coat a
6 x 9 inch (15 x 23 cm) brownie pan with coconut flour.*

Cake
In a bowl, whisk eggs, egg white and sweetener until
light and airy. Add water to the egg mixture. If using
vanilla extract, add this now. In a separate bowl, combine
coconut flour with baking powder and—if using—vanilla
powder. Add the dry ingredients to the batter and whisk
until smooth.

Pour batter into the prepared brownie pan and bake at
350°F (175°C) for about 15 minutes. Let cool completely
on wire rack.

Frosting
In a saucepan melt butter with sweetener stirring until
sweetener is completely dissolved.

Gently whisk egg yolk into the lukewarm mixture and
immediately cover the cake with the frosting. Garnish the
top with a generous sprinkling of grated coconut. Keep
refrigerated.

To serve, cut into desired portions.

Tiger Marble Cake

SERVES 14

Ingredients:

⅔ cup (150 g) unsalted butter, melted and cooled

5 large eggs

3 tbsp erythritol powder and ⅛ tsp stevia powder

1 cup (200 ml) whipping cream

½ cup (100 ml) coconut flour

½ cup (100 ml) almond flour

2 tsp baking powder

1 tsp vanilla powder or 2 tsp pure vanilla extract

2 tbsp cocoa powder

METHOD:

Preheat oven to 350°F (175°C). Line a 6 cup (1½ liter) loaf pan with parchment paper. Melt and cool butter.

In a bowl, beat eggs and sweetener until light and airy. Add cooled butter and cream to egg mixture and whisk. If using vanilla extract, add this now.

In a separate bowl, mix dry ingredients with—if using—vanilla powder. Stir dry mixture into batter.

In a separate bowl, pour a third of the batter and add the cocoa powder.

Pour half of the light-colored batter into the prepared loaf pan, then add the brown batter, and top off with the rest of the light-colored batter. With a fork, lift up some batter from the bottom so as to create a marbled effect.

Bake on center rack at 350°F (175°C) for about 30 minutes. The cake is ready when a toothpick inserted in the center comes out clean.

➤ TIP: **For nut allergies:** Exchange almond flour for 3 tbsp coconut flour.

Strawberry and Vanilla Cream Lengths

MAKES 2 LENGTHS

Vanilla Cream
3 large egg yolks
1 tbsp erythritol powder and $\frac{1}{16}$ tsp stevia powder
½ cup (100 ml) whipping cream
½ tsp vanilla powder or seeds from ½ vanilla bean or 1 tsp pure vanilla extract
3½ tbsp (50 g) very soft butter

Lengths
¼ cup (60 g) unsalted butter
8 large eggs + 1 egg yolk
6 tbsp erythritol powder and $\frac{1}{16}$ tsp stevia powder
¾ cup (200 ml) coconut flour
2 tsp ground cardamom
2 tsp baking powder

Garnish
small container of fresh strawberries
1 egg white
slivered almonds

METHOD:

Preheat oven to 350°F (175°C). Line a cookie sheet with parchment paper. Melt and cool butter. Make vanilla cream.

Vanilla Cream
In a saucepan, mix all the ingredients except for the butter. Bring to a simmer. Simmer while stirring continuously until cream thickens. *Do not let cream come to a boil.* Let cool.

Add in the butter, little by little. Keep cream refrigerated. The cream can be made a day ahead.

Length
Whisk eggs, yolk, and sweetener until light and airy. Stir the cooled butter into egg mixture.

Combine coconut flour with the cardamom and baking powder. Work the dry ingredients into the batter. Let dough rest as it will rise some.

Divide dough in half into two lengths, and place them on the prepared cookie sheet. Flatten the lengths down the middle, and make a small indentation along the entire length. *Do not make the dough too thin.* Place vanilla cream in the indentation, and top with sliced fresh strawberries. Brush edges with whipped egg white then sprinkle with slivered almonds.

Bake at 350°F (175°C) for 20 to 30 minutes. Cool on wire rack.

◆▶ **TIP:** For a delicious variation use fresh or frozen blueberries.

For a less "eggy" vanilla cream replace one yolk with ½ a sheet of gelatin (½ tsp powder).

To handle sticky dough more easily, wet palms with cold water.

Cinnamon Length

SERVES 10–12

Ingredients:

Dough
2 tbsp (30 g) unsalted butter, melted and cooled
4 large eggs + 1 egg yolk
3 tbsp erythritol powder and ⅛ tsp stevia powder
½ cup (100 ml) coconut flour
½ tbsp ground cardamom
1 tsp baking powder

Filling
¼ cup (50 g) unsalted butter
½ (100 ml) cup almond flour
½ tsp vanilla powder or 1 tsp pure vanilla extract
1 tbsp cinnamon
2 tbsp erythritol powder and ¹⁄₁₆ tsp stevia powder

Garnish
1 egg white
slivered almonds

METHOD:

Preheat oven to 350°F (175°C). Line a cookie sheet with parchment paper. Melt butter. Make filling.

Dough
Whisk eggs, yolk, and sweetener until light and airy. Mix in the cooled butter.
Combine coconut flour with cardamom and baking powder and work into the batter.

Filling
Melt butter and mix in the remaining ingredients.
Flatten the dough into a rectangle on the parchment paper. Drizzle or spread filling over the rectangle.
Fold the dough over or gently roll it, nudging the sides upwards, making the roll higher. Brush with whipped egg white and sprinkle with slivered almonds. Bake at 350°F (175°C) for about 30 minutes. Cool on wire rack.

➤ **TIP:** Omit filling, and this becomes a coconut version of a classic Swedish wheat length.
To handle sticky dough more easily dust hands with coconut flour, or wet palms with cold water.

53

Fat Tuesday Buns—
Swedish Mardi Gras Buns

MAKES 4 LARGE BUNS

Ingredients:

Buns
¼ cup (50 g) unsalted butter,
  melted and cooled
4 large eggs
3 tbsp erythritol powder and ⅛ tsp
  stevia powder
½ cup (100 ml) whipping cream
¼ cup (50 ml) coconut flour
4 tbsp psyllium husk
2 tsp baking powder
1 tsp ground cardamom

Almond Paste
½ cup (150 ml) almonds
2 tbsp erythritol powder and ⅛ tsp
  stevia powder
1–2 tbsp whipping cream

Garnish
whipped cream
powdered sweetener

METHOD:

*Blanch and grind almonds. Preheat oven to 350° (175°C).
Line cookie sheet with parchment paper. Melt butter.*

Buns
Beat eggs and sweetener several minutes until light and
airy. Add cream and cooled butter to egg mixture. In a
bowl, mix dry ingredients and work this into the batter,
leaving no lumps. Let dough rest as it will rise some.

   Moisten palms with cold water and shape 4 nicely
rounded buns. Place buns on prepared cookie sheet and
bake at 350°F (175°C) for about 25 minutes. Cool completely on wire rack.

Almond Paste
Blanch almonds. Remove skins by rubbing almonds
between kitchen towels. Dry almonds thoroughly.

   Grind almonds with a nut grinder or pulse almonds
in a coffee or Magic Bullet-type grinder. In a food processor pulse ground almonds with sweetener several
minutes. Add the cream, little by little, until you reach
the desired consistency.

How to Assemble a Fat Tuesday Bun:
Cut a triangular lid in the top of the bun. Scoop out
some of the crumb so as to leave a hollow. Mix crumb
with the prepared almond paste, adding additional
cream if needed, to get a smooth paste. Fill the hollow
with almond paste and cover with a generous dollop
of whipped cream. Place the lid back on the bun. Dust
with powdered sweetener.

Chocolate Cupcakes

SERVES 12

Ingredients:

Cupcakes
⅔ cup (150 g) unsalted butter
4 large eggs
3 tbsp erythritol powder and ⅛ tsp stevia powder
½ cup (100 ml) crème fraîche
½ tsp vanilla powder or 1 tsp pure vanilla extract
½ cup (100 ml) coconut flour
½ cup (100 ml) almond flour
2 tsp baking powder
4 tbsp cocoa powder

Chocolate Frosting
7 tbsp (100 g) very soft unsalted butter
3 tbsp erythritol powder and ⅛ tsp stevia powder
½ tsp vanilla powder or 1 tsp pure vanilla extract
4 tbsp (50 ml) cocoa powder
1¾ oz (50 g) cream cheese

METHOD:

Preheat oven to 350°F (175°C). Place large cupcake liners in a cupcake pan. Melt butter.

Cupcakes
Beat eggs and sweetener until light and airy. Add cooled butter and crème fraîche—and vanilla extract if using—to egg mixture.

In a separate bowl, mix dry ingredients with—if using—vanilla powder, and stir thoroughly into the batter.

Fill prepared cupcake liners to ¾ full. Bake at 350°F (175°C) for about 15 minutes.

Cool completely on wire rack.

Chocolate Frosting
Blend ingredients thoroughly until creamy and free of lumps. Pipe or spread frosting onto cupcakes and dust with cocoa.

TIP: For Chocolate Mocha Cupcakes, add instant coffee granules to batter and filling.

58

Hazelnut Filbert Cupcakes

SERVES 12

Ingredients:

Cupcakes
⅔ cup (150 g) unsalted butter
6 large eggs
2 tbsp erythritol powder and ¹⁄₁₆ tsp
    stevia powder
3½ oz (100 g) cream cheese
1 tsp vanilla powder or 1 tsp pure
    vanilla extract
⅓ cup (75 ml) coconut flour
2 tbsp psyllium husk
¼ cup (50 ml) cocoa powder
2 tsp baking powder

Frosting
½ cup (100 ml) chopped hazelnuts
    (filberts)
7 tbsp (100 g) soft unsalted butter
1¾ oz (50 g) cream cheese
3 tbsp erythritol powder and ¹⁄₁₆ tsp
    stevia powder

Garnish
chopped hazelnuts (filberts)

METHOD:

Preheat oven to 350°F (175°C). Place large cupcake liners in cupcake pan. Melt butter.

Cupcakes
Beat eggs and sweetener until light and airy. Add melted butter, cream cheese, and vanilla extract or powder. Beat until smooth.

In a separate bowl, mix dry ingredients thoroughly. Add to batter, blending thoroughly to remove any lumps.

Fill prepared cupcake liners ¾ full.

Bake at 350°F (175°C) for about 15–20 minutes. Cool completely on wire rack.

Frosting
Blend ingredients until smooth.

Spread or pipe frosting over cupcakes. Sprinkle with chopped hazelnuts.

Coconut Cupcakes

SERVES 12

Ingredients:

Cupcakes
⅔ cup (150 g) unsalted butter
1¾ oz (50 g) high-quality dark chocolate, minimum 70% cocoa content
6 large eggs
2 tbsp erythritol powder and ¹⁄₁₆ tsp stevia powder
3½ oz (100 g) cream cheese
2 tbsp psyllium husk
⅓ cup (75 ml) coconut flour
1 tsp vanilla powder or 2 tsp pure vanilla extract
2 tsp baking powder

Frosting
½ cup (100 ml) whipping cream
3 tbsp erythritol powder and ⅛ tsp (75 ml) stevia powder
½ tsp vanilla powder or 1 tsp pure vanilla extract
2 cups (150 ml) coconut flakes, unsweetened
1 egg yolk
7 tbsp (100 g) soft unsalted butter

Garnish
coconut chips, unsweetened

METHOD:

Preheat oven to 350°F (175°C). Place large liners in cupcake pan. Melt butter with chocolate.

Cupcakes
Beat eggs and sweetener until light and airy. Whisk in chocolate, butter, and cream cheese. Continue whisking until obtaining a smooth batter. If using vanilla extract add this now. In a separate bowl, mix dry ingredients with—if using—vanilla powder. Mix thoroughly to obtain a lump-free batter.

Fill cupcake liners ¾ full and bake on center rack at 350°F (175°C) for 15–20 minutes. Cool completely on wire rack.

Frosting
In a saucepan, bring cream, sweetener, coconut flakes and vanilla powder or extract to a boil. Simmer 2 to 3 minutes. Stir occasionally until sweetener is completely dissolved. Let cool.

Beat in egg yolk and butter, in batches, to the cooled cream.

Frost the cupcakes generously and sprinkle with unsweetened coconut chips.

Lemon Whoopie Pies

SERVES 10

Ingredients:

Cakes
7 tbsp (100 g) unsalted butter
3 large eggs
3 tbsp erythritol powder and ⅛ tsp
   stevia powder
¼ cup (50 ml) crème fraîche
½ cup (100 ml) coconut flour
½ cup (100 ml) almond flour
½ tsp vanilla powder or 1 tsp pure
   vanilla extract
1½ tsp baking powder
juice of one lemon

Lemon Cream
3 tbsp erythritol powder and ⅛ tsp
   stevia powder
7 tbsp (100 g) very soft unsalted
   butter
1¾ oz (50 g) full-fat cream cheese
grated zest from one lemon

METHOD:

Preheat oven to 350°F (175°C). Zest and juice lemon. Melt butter. Line cookie sheet with parchment paper.

Cakes
Beat eggs and sweetener until light and airy. Beat in crème fraîche and lemon juice, add the melted butter and vanilla extract, if using. Mix thoroughly.

In a separate bowl, mix dry ingredients with—if using—vanilla powder. Stir into the batter.

With the help of a tablespoon, scoop out and shape 20 round cakes of equal size. Place cakes on prepared cookie sheet and bake at 350°F (175°C) for 10 to 15 minutes. The cakes are ready when a toothpick inserted in the center comes out clean. Place cookie sheet on wire rack and leave cakes on rack until completely cooled.

Lemon Cream
Mix the ingredients until smooth and creamy.

Sandwich the cakes together two and two with a generous layer of cream. Keep refrigerated.

◆▶ **TIP:** Vary by replacing lemon with lime.

Experiment to discover different favorite cake/frosting combinations.

Coconut Whoopie Pies

SERVES 10

Ingredients:

Cakes
7 tbsp (100 g) unsalted butter
3 large eggs
3 tbsp erythritol powder and ⅛ tsp
    stevia powder
¼ cup (50 ml) crème fraîche
½ cup (100 ml) coconut flour
½ cup (100 ml) almond flour
4 tbsp (50 ml) cocoa powder
½ tsp vanilla powder or 1 tsp pure
    vanilla extract
1½ tsp baking powder

Coconut Cream
½ cup (100 ml) whipping cream
3 tbsp erythritol powder and ⅛ tsp
    stevia powder
2¾ cups (200 ml) coconut flakes,
    unsweetened
7 tbsp (100 g) soft unsalted butter
½ tsp vanilla powder or 1 tsp pure
    vanilla extract
1 egg yolk

METHOD:

Preheat oven to 350°F (175°C). Melt butter. Line cookie sheet with parchment paper.

Cakes
Beat eggs and sweetener until light and airy. Add crème fraîche while whisking. Pour in melted butter and vanilla extract, if using. Mix well.

In a separate bowl, mix dry ingredients with—if using—vanilla powder. Add to the batter and blend thoroughly.

With the help of a tablespoon, scoop out 20 equally-sized round cakes. Place cakes on prepared cookie sheet and bake at 350°F (175°C) for 10 to 15 minutes. Cakes are ready when a toothpick inserted in center comes out clean. Set cookie sheet on wire rack and leave cakes to cool on sheet.

Coconut Cream
In a saucepan, bring cream, sweetener, and coconut flakes to a boil. Let simmer for 2 to 3 minutes. Stir occasionally while letting the sweetener dissolve completely. Add vanilla powder or extract. Cool at room temperature.

To the cooled cream add butter and yolk in batches, blending well between additions. Stir thoroughly.

Sandwich the cooled cakes together, two and two, with a generous layer of cream.

◆→TIP: Keep refrigerated.
Experiment with different cake/frosting combinations to discover new favorites.

Lavender Chocolate Whoopie Pies

SERVES 10

Ingredients:

Cakes
7 tbsp (100 g) unsalted butter
3 large eggs
3 tbsp erythritol powder and
⅛ tsp stevia powder
¼ cup (50 ml) crème fraîche
½ cup (100 ml) coconut flour
½ cup (100 ml) almond flour
1½ tsp baking powder
1 tsp vanilla powder or 2 tsp pure
vanilla extract

Chocolate Cream
½ cup (100 ml) whipping cream
7 lavender flowers (optional)
1 egg yolk
½ tsp vanilla powder or 1 tsp pure
vanilla extract
1¾ oz (50 g) high-quality dark
chocolate, minimum 70%
cocoa content
7 tbsp (100 g) very soft unsalted
butter

METHOD:

Preheat oven to 350°F (175°C). Melt butter. Line cookie sheet with parchment paper.

Cakes
Beat eggs and sweetener until light and airy. Add crème fraîche while continuing to whisk. Blend in cooled butter and vanilla extract if using. Mix well.

In a separate bowl, mix dry ingredients, adding vanilla powder if using. Incorporate into the batter thoroughly.

With a tablespoon scoop out and shape 20 equally-sized round cakes. Place cakes on the prepared baking sheet and bake at 350°F (175°C) for 10 to 15 minutes. The cakes are ready when a toothpick inserted in the center comes out clean. Place the cookie sheet on a wire rack and leave cookies to cool on the sheet.

Chocolate Cream
In a saucepan, quickly bring cream and lavender flowers to a boil. Simmer the mixture a few minutes and then remove from heat. Let the lavender flowers steep about 5 minutes in the cooling cream. Strain the cooled cream, then return it to the saucepan and whisk in the egg yolk and vanilla powder or extract. Let simmer until cream starts to thicken—*do not bring to a boil!*

While whisking, add chocolate pieces to the cream, and then blend in the very soft butter.

Sandwich the completely cooled cakes together with a generous amount of cream.

TIP: Keep refrigerated.
Experiment with different cake/frosting combinations to discover new favorites.

LAYER CAKES, PIES, AND CRUMBLES

Budapest Cream Roll

SERVES 6

Ingredients:

Cake Layer
6 large egg whites, at room
   temperature
3 tbsp erythritol powder and ⅛ tsp
   stevia powder
¼ cup (50 ml) coconut flour
½ cup (100 ml) finely chopped
   hazelnuts (filberts)
½ cup (100 ml) hazelnut flour

Filling
1–1½ cup (200–300 ml) whipping
   cream
¾ cup (200–300 ml) raspberries

Garnish
2–3 squares high-quality dark
   chocolate, melted. *Optional*: Mix
   chocolate with 2 tsp unsalted
   butter or coconut fat.

METHOD:

*Remove eggs from refrigerator. Preheat oven to 350°F (175°C).
Line a 10 x 12 inch (25 x 30 cm) cookie sheet with parchment
paper.*

Cake Layer
Beat egg whites until soft peaks form. Gradually add
sweetener and beat until stiff peaks form. In a separate
bowl, combine coconut and hazelnut flour. Add finely
chopped nuts. Using a figure-eight motion gently fold the
flour/nut mixture into the egg whites.

   Spread batter onto prepared cookie sheet and bake at
350°F (175°C) for about 15 minutes. Turn cake layer onto a
clean sheet of parchment paper. Remove baking paper and
leave cake layer to cool on wire rack.

Filling
Whip cream until soft peaks form. Fold in fresh or semi-
thawed raspberries. Spread filling over cake layer and
gently roll up Swiss Roll-fashion. As garnish, drizzle the
roll with dark chocolate mixture. To serve, cut the roll into
6 slices.

◆► TIP: Use eggs at room temperature. Start beating at
medium speed. Increase speed and add sweetener gradually once soft peaks have formed.

Chocolate Pie

SERVES 10–12

Ingredients:

Pie Crust
½ cup unsalted butter (125 g)
2 large eggs
3 tbsp erythritol powder and ⅛ tsp
  stevia powder
⅔ cup (150 ml) coconut flour
2 tsp baking powder
½ tsp vanilla powder or 1 tsp pure
  vanilla extract

Filling
3½ oz (100 g) high-quality dark
  chocolate, preferably at least
  70% cocoa content
2 large eggs
10½ oz (300 g) cream cheese

To Serve
whipped cream
1 passion fruit per person

METHOD:

Preheat oven to 350°F (175°C). Melt butter.

Pie Crust
Beat eggs and sweetener until light and airy. Add cooled butter and—if using—vanilla extract to the egg mixture.

In a separate bowl, mix dry ingredients and—if using—add vanilla powder. Mix into the batter. Knead dough smooth.

Cover the bottom of an 8–9 inch (21–24 cm) tart or a springform pan with the dough.

Filling
Melt chocolate by placing it in a bowl placed over a pan of simmering water. Be careful not to allow any water moisture into the bowl.

Whisk eggs with the cream cheese until smooth. Incorporate melted chocolate and blend well. Pour filling over pie crust.

Bake at 350°F (175°C) for about 30 minutes. Touch surface to make sure filling has settled.

Serve the lukewarm pie with a dollop of whipped cream and a passion fruit cut into halves.

▸ **TIP:** The filling may need additional sweetener if the cocoa content is higher than 70%. Passion fruit makes a superb addition to a serving of this pie.

Lemon and Lime Pie

SERVES 8–10

Ingredients:

Pie Crust
½ cup (125 g) unsalted butter
2 large eggs
3 tbsp erythritol powder and
    ¹⁄₁₆ tsp stevia powder
⅔ cup (150 ml) coconut flour
2 tsp baking powder
½ tsp vanilla powder or 1 tsp pure
    vanilla extract

Filling
3 large eggs
3 tbsp erythritol powder and
    ¹⁄₁₆ tsp stevia powder
1¼ cup (200 ml) crème fraîche
zest and juice of one lime
zest and juice of one lemon
½ tsp vanilla powder or 1 tsp pure
    vanilla extract

To Serve
lightly whipped cream

METHOD:

Preheat oven to 350°F (175°C). Zest and juice lime and lemon. Melt butter.

Pie Crust
Beat eggs and sweetener until light and airy. Stir the melted, cooled butter into egg mixture. If using, add vanilla extract to the batter.

Mix coconut flour with baking powder and—if using—vanilla powder. Add to the batter, making a dough.

Cover bottom of an 8–9 inch (21–24 cm) tart or springform pan with the dough.

Filling
Whisk eggs and sweetener. Add in crème fraîche, zest and juice from the lime and lemon. Add vanilla powder or extract.

Pour filling over the prepared pie crust and bake at 350°F (175°C) for about 30 minutes. Watch carefully and remove pie before filling has fully settled. The filling continues to firm up as it cools.

➤ **TIP:** This pie—with a dollop of lightly whipped cream—is equally good served lukewarm or cold.

Queen of Pies

SERVES 8–10

Ingredients:

Pie Crust
½ cup (125 g) unsalted butter
2 large eggs
3 tbsp erythritol powder and ¹⁄₁₆ tsp
    stevia powder
½ cup (100 ml) coconut flour
1–2 oz (50–100 ml) chopped
    almonds
2 tsp baking powder
½ tsp vanilla powder or 1 tsp pure
    vanilla extract

Filling
3 large eggs
3 tbsp erythritol powder and ¹⁄₁₆ tsp
    stevia powder
½ tsp vanilla powder or 1 tsp pure
    vanilla extract
10½ oz (300 g) full-fat cream
    cheese
¾ cup (200 ml) raspberries
½ cup (100 ml) blueberries

To Serve
lightly whipped cream

METHOD:

Preheat oven to 350°F (175°C). Melt butter. Drain berries if using frozen.

Pie Crust
Beat eggs and sweetener until light and airy. Add melted and cooled butter to the egg mixture. Add vanilla extract if using.

In a separate bowl, mix coconut flour, baking powder and—if using—vanilla powder. Stir in chopped almonds. Add mixture to the batter and work into a dough.

Cover bottom of an 8–9 inch (21–24 cm) tart or springform pan with the dough.

Filling
Whisk eggs, sweetener, vanilla, and cream cheese together, eliminating any lumps. Gently fold in raspberries and blueberries.

Pour filling over pie crust and bake at 350°F (175°C) for about 30 minutes. Remove pie from oven before filling is fully settled. It will firm up as it cools.

Serve pie either lukewarm or cold accompanied by lightly whipped cream.

➤**TIP:** This cake is best made with fresh berries as frozen might make the cake too moist. If you must use frozen berries, add an extra egg, and drain the berries thoroughly.

76

Classic Swedish Cream Cake

Ingredients:

Cake
¾ cup + 2 tbsp (200 g) unsalted butter
7 large eggs
3 tbsp erythritol powder and ¹⁄₁₆ tsp stevia powder
½ tsp vanilla powder or 1 tsp pure vanilla extract
⅔ cup (150 ml) whipping cream
¾ cup (200 ml) coconut flour
2½ tsp baking powder

Crushed Berry Layer
1 cup (200–300 ml) lightly mashed strawberries
½–1 cup (100–200 ml) whipped whipping cream (optional)

Vanilla Cream
1 gelatin leaf or equivalent in Knox gelatin powder
1 cup (200 ml) whipped cream
3 large eggs yolks
2 tbsp erythritol powder and ¹⁄₁₆ tsp stevia powder
½ tsp vanilla powder, or seeds from 1 vanilla bean, split and seeds scraped or 1 tsp pure vanilla extract
7 tbsp (100 g) unsalted butter, softened

Garnish
1–1½ cups (200–300 ml) whipping cream
fresh strawberries

METHOD:

Preheat oven to 350°F (350°C). Line a 9 inch (24 cm) springform pan with parchment paper, or butter and coat lightly with coconut flour. Melt butter. Crush berries and—if using—whip cream for berry layer. Make vanilla cream—preferably a day ahead.

Cake
Beat eggs and sweetener until light and airy. Add melted and cooled butter to the egg mixture.

Add vanilla powder *or* extract, and the whipping cream.

Combine coconut flour and baking powder well, mashing any lumps. Stir into the batter.

Pour batter into the prepared pan and bake at 350°F (175°C) for approximately 30 minutes. The cake is done when a toothpick inserted in the center comes out clean.

Vanilla Cream
This cream is best made one day ahead.

Soak the gelatin leaf in cold water for at least 5 minutes, or follow instructions for gelatin powder.

In a saucepan, whisk together remaining ingredients, except for the butter. Simmer—*do not bring to a boil*—until cream starts to thicken. Remove from heat and add prepared gelatin. Gradually stir in the butter.

Refrigerate cream, stirring now and then. The cream will continue to thicken as long as it is kept cold.

Cut cake into three layers. Spread vanilla cream over bottom layer. Place second layer on top of the cream, and cover it with lightly crushed strawberries. Place last layer carefully on the berries. Generously pipe or spread whipped cream so as to cover entire cake. Garnish with fresh strawberries

TIP: Vanilla powder tints the vanilla cream slightly brown; the seeds from a vanilla bean will not do this.

Strawberry is the traditional filling in a classic Swedish Cream Cake but the cake is equally scrumptious with either raspberries and blueberries. Keep in mind, blueberries stain your guests' mouths blue, perhaps not such a good idea at large parties or more important celebrations.

TIP: Freeze leftover egg whites for later use in, for example, a Budapest Roll.

Raspberry Mousse Cake

SERVES 10–12

Ingredients:

Mazarin Layer
1⅓ cups (200 g) almonds
3 tbsp erythritol powder and
⅛ tsp stevia powder
3 to 4 tbsp whipping cream
⅔ cup (150 g) soft butter
3 large eggs
3 tbsp coconut flour

Raspberry Mousse
8 gelatin leaves or equivalent in
Knox Gelatin Powder
2 cups (500 g) raspberries
2 cups (500 ml) whipping
cream
3 tbsp erythritol powder and
¹⁄₁₆ tsp stevia powder

For Serving
fresh raspberries
lemon balm

METHOD:

Preheat oven to 350°F (175°C). Layer a 9 inch (24 cm) springform pan with parchment paper. Blanch and skin almonds. Dry thoroughly.

Mazarin Layer
Grind the thoroughly dried almonds in a nut grinder or pulse in a coffee or Magic Bullet-type grinder.

In a food processor pulse ground almonds and sweetener several minutes. Add cream, a little at a time, until right consistency is reached.

With the almond paste in the food processor add butter and pulse. Add eggs, one at a time, and mix until smooth. Stir in flour by hand.

Spoon almond paste batter evenly into the prepared springform pan and bake at 350°F (175°C) for approximately 20 minutes. Place springform pan on a wire rack and leave cake to cool completely in the pan. When cake has cooled, remove parchment paper and return the cake layer to the pan.

Raspberry Mousse
Leave gelatin leaves to soak in cold water at least 5 minutes *or* prepare gelatin powder according to instructions on packet.

Purée raspberries. In a saucepan, pour ½ cup (100 ml) of the raspberry purée and heat through. Add whipping cream and sweetener, mixing well. Stirring, add prepared gelatin to the saucepan with hot raspberry mix. Mix hot raspberry mixture with rest of purée.

Spread mousse over cake layer. Leave to harden in freezer at least 4 hours. Remove cake from freezer 1 hour before serving. Loosen the edges of the half-thawed cake with a sharp knife. Garnish with fresh raspberries and lemon balm.

➤ TIP: If cake is made a day in advance, or kept in the freezer for a longer period, thaw it slowly in the refrigerator over 10 to 12 hours. Or, remove cake from the freezer in the morning if it is to be eaten that night.

Lime and Strawberry Mousse Cake

SERVES 14–16

Ingredients:

Chocolate Cake
⅔ cup (150 g) unsalted butter
4 large eggs
2 tbsp erythritol powder and
⅟₁₆ tsp stevia powder
½ cup (100 ml) whipping cream
⅔ cup (150 ml) coconut flour
4 tbsp (50 ml) cocoa powder
1 tsp vanilla powder or 2 tsp
pure vanilla extract

Lime Mousse
4 gelatin leaves or equivalent in
Knox Gelatin Powder
½ cup (100 ml) crème fraîche
½ cup (100 ml) Greek yogurt
3 tbsp erythritol powder and
⅛ tsp stevia powder
zest and juice of three limes
1 cup (200 ml) whipping cream

Strawberry Mousse
6 gelatin leaves or equivalent in
Knox Gelatin Powder
2 cups (500 g) strawberries
2 tbsp erythritol powder and
⅟₁₆ tsp stevia powder
1⅓ cups (300 ml) whipping
cream

Garnish
fresh strawberries
limes

METHOD:

Preheat oven to 350°F (175°C). Line bottom of a 9 inch (24 cm) springform pan with parchment paper. Melt butter. Zest and juice limes. Whip cream for lime and strawberry mousse.

Chocolate Cake
Beat eggs and sweetener until light and airy. Whisk in the melted, cooled butter. Still whisking, add the cream. If using vanilla extract, add this now.

In a separate bowl, mix coconut flour, cocoa powder, and—if using—vanilla powder.

Blend the mixture into batter until smooth.

Spoon the batter into prepared springform pan and bake at 350°F (175°C) for approximately 15 minutes. The cake is ready when a toothpick inserted in the center comes out clean. Cool cake in the pan. Remove parchment paper, but return the cake to the pan.

Lime Mousse
If using gelatin leaves, soak them in cold water at least 5 minutes. Follow directions on packet for gelatin powder. Blend crème fraîche, Greek yogurt, sweetener, and lime zest thoroughly. In a saucepan heat lime juice and dissolve the gelatin leaves or prepared powder. Remove from heat and cool. Add cooled lime juice to crème fraîche mixture and gently fold in whipped cream. Cover chocolate cake layer with lime mousse and place in freezer several hours. Note: Do not remove cake from pan. Butter pan edges to make mousse easier to remove.

Strawberry Mousse
Prepare gelatin as for Lime Mousse. Purée strawberries using a hand blender. In a saucepan, heat ½ cup (100 ml) of strawberry purée together with the sweetener. Melt gelatin in the hot purée, stirring well. Remove from heat and let cool.

Mix gelatin mixture with the rest of the strawberry purée. Gently fold whipped cream into the purée.

Remove cake from freezer and cover the frozen lime mousse with strawberry mousse. Return cake to the freezer for another 3 hours or place in the refrigerator for at least 5 hours.

Remove cake from freezer 1 to 2 hours before serving. If the cake has spent a longer time frozen defrost it slowly in the refrigerator over 10 to 12 hours.

To serve, garnish with strawberries and lime segments.

TIP: The smaller pan you use, the taller the cake. To increase the height, wrap doubled-up parchment paper all around the pan, overlap edges and secure. Carefully spread mousse inside and up, taking care that the paper doesn't give way.

Midsummer Pie

SERVES 8–10

Ingredients:

Pie Crust

½ cup (125 g) unsalted butter

2 large eggs

2 tbsp erythritol powder and ¹⁄₁₆ tsp
  stevia powder

⅔ cup (150 ml) coconut flour

2 tsp baking powder

½ tsp vanilla powder or 1 tsp pure
  vanilla extract

Vanilla Ice Custard

1 gelatin leaf or equivalent in Knox
  Gelatin Powder

1 cup (200 ml) whipping cream

3 large egg yolks

1½ tsp vanilla powder, or seeds
  from ½ vanilla bean or 3 tsp
  pure vanilla extract

2 tbsp erythritol powder and ¹⁄₁₆ tsp
  stevia powder

7 tbsp (100 g) unsalted butter,
  softened

2 cups (500 g) sliced fresh
  strawberries

Jellied Strawberry Glaze

4 gelatin leaves or equivalent in
  Knox Gelatin Powder

¾ cup (200 ml) water

a lightly squeezed lemon

2 tbsp erythritol powder and ¹⁄₁₆ tsp
  stevia powder

½ cup (100 ml) frozen strawberries

METHOD:

Make Vanilla Custard a day ahead.
Preheat oven to 350°F (175°C). Melt butter.

Pie Crust

Beat eggs with sweetener until light and airy. Add melted and cooled butter, and if using vanilla extract add this now. In a separate bowl, combine coconut flour with baking powder and—if using—vanilla powder. Add to the batter, pressing out any lumps, and working mixture into a dough.

Line bottom and sides of an 8–9 inch (21–24 cm) spring-form pan with the dough. Press dough up the sides at least 1 inch. If using the smaller-sized pan, press dough further up the sides, so as to contain the filling. Dust your fingers with coconut flour to help with sticky dough. The crust will not slide down so there is no need to make an overhang. Bake crust at 350°F (175°C) for about 10 minutes. Let cool on wire rack.

Vanilla Ice Custard (*preferably made one day in ahead*)

Soak gelatin leaves in cold water for at least 5 minutes or prepare powdered gelatin according to package instructions. In a saucepan, bring remaining ingredients—except butter—to a simmer. Simmer, all the while whisking, until the cream starts to thicken. *Do not bring to a boil*. Remove pan from heat and add the gelatin to dissolve. Add butter a little at a time.

Jellied Strawberry Glaze

Soak gelatin as for the vanilla custard.

Bring water, lemon, sweetener, and strawberries to a boil. The strawberries shall become a bit mushy. Strain mixture through double cheesecloth; preparation (except gelatin) up to this point can be done a day ahead.

Heat the juice and stir in the gelatin to dissolve. Store jelly cold, preferably in the freezer, 5 to 10 minutes. Check often so the jelly doesn't set completely. If it happens, reheat very gently.

Cover cold pie crust with vanilla ice custard and a layer of sliced fresh strawberries. Spoon the semi-set strawberry glaze over the strawberries. Refrigerate.

TIP: To give the vanilla ice custard time to thicken, make it a day ahead. Refrigerate and let the cream thicken overnight. To save even more time, make a large batch of strawberry juice and freeze in 1-cup jars. That way, just thaw desired quantity and heat before adding gelatin.

Simple Mocha Cake

SERVES 10–12

Ingredients:

Cake
3 large eggs
3 tbsp erythritol powder and ¹⁄₁₆ tsp
    stevia powder
7 tbsp (100 g) unsalted butter,
    softened
½ cup (100 ml) whipping cream
¼ cup (50 ml) coconut flour
¾ cup (200 ml) ground hazelnuts
    (filberts)
1½ tsp baking powder
½ tsp vanilla powder or 1 tsp pure
    vanilla extract

Mocha Cream
3 large egg yolks
3 tbsp erythritol powder and ⅛ tsp
    stevia powder
½ tsp vanilla powder or 1 tsp pure
    vanilla extract
3 tsp instant coffee granules
⅔ cup (150 ml) whipping cream
1 cup (225 g) unsalted butter,
    softened

Garnish
raw chocolate

METHOD:

Preheat oven to 350°F (175°C). Line a 9 inch (24 cm) spring-form pan with parchment paper or butter it and coat lightly with coconut flour.

Cake
Beat eggs with sweetener until light and airy. Melt butter with the cream and whisk butter-cream mixture into the egg batter. If using vanilla extract, add this now.

In a separate bowl, mix dry ingredients and—if using—vanilla powder, then add it to the batter.

Pour batter into prepared pan and bake at 350°F (175°C) for 10–15 minutes. Let cool and cut the cake into two layers.

Mocha Cream
In a saucepan, while whisking, bring the egg yolks, sweetener, vanilla powder or extract, instant coffee, and cream to a simmer. Simmer, stirring constantly until cream starts to thicken. *Do not bring to a boil.* Remove saucepan from heat and let mixture cool some.

Add butter, a little at a time. Refrigerate, stirring occasionally. The cream thickens as it chills.

Sandwich the two cake layers with a third of the cream, leaving the rest for frosting top of the cake. Sprinkle cake liberally with coarsely grated raw chocolate. Keep cake refrigerated.

◆➤**TIP:** To make neat, even cake layers, cut with a piece of sewing thread.

Blueberry Crumble

SERVES 4–6

Ingredients:

1⅓ cup (300 ml) blueberries
¾ cup + 2 tbsp (200 g) unsalted
    butter
3 tbsp erythritol powder and
    ⅛ tsp stevia powder
2 oz (100 ml) chopped almonds
¼ cup (50 ml) coconut flour
⅔ cup (150 ml) almond flour
½ cup (100 ml) hazelnut (filberts)
    flour
ground cinnamon (optional)

METHOD:

Preheat oven to 390°F (200°C).

Place blueberries in an ovenproof dish and sprinkle with ½ tbsp ground cinnamon (optional).

In a saucepan, melt butter with sweetener, letting it dissolve properly. Add chopped almonds.

Combine coconut flour with almond and hazelnut flour, mashing to remove lumps. Stir flours into the butter mixture. Spread the butter-flour mixture over the berries—it will crumble when baking. Bake at 390°F (200°C) for about 15 minutes—check often to make sure the top doesn't burn. The crumble should be juicy and have nice color.

Serve the crumble with a delicious homemade vanilla custard!

➤ **TIP:** Replace the blueberries with rhubarb if you have them. Sweeten rhubarb with 3 tbsp erythritol powder and ⅛ tsp stevia powder, or as needed.

As a change, try dusting the crumble with a tablespoon of cinnamon.

Vanilla Custard

SERVES 4

Ingredients:

4 large egg yolks
3 tbsp erythritol powder and
    ⅛ tsp stevia powder
1⅓ cups (300 ml) whipping cream
½ vanilla bean or ½ tsp vanilla
    powder (tints custard brown)
    or 1 tsp pure vanilla extract
1½ tbsp (20 g) unsalted butter
½ cup (100 ml) whipping cream
    (optional)

METHOD:

The vanilla custard can be made a day ahead.

Whisk the egg yolks with the sweetener. In a saucepan bring the cream to boil with either vanilla seeds and the hollowed bean, vanilla powder or vanilla extract. Let boil a few minutes. Remove the saucepan from heat.

Remove the vanilla pod. Pour the hot—but not boiling—vanilla cream into the egg mixture while whisking . Put the mixture back in the saucepan.

Simmer the custard until it starts to thicken. Bring it near to boiling, *but do not boil* or the custard will curdle.

Once the custard has thickened, remove pan from the heat and stir in the butter little by little. Refrigerate immediately.

Just before serving, whip the cream fairly stiff and fold into the vanilla custard.

American Pancakes

SERVES 6

Ingredients:

¼ cup (50 g) unsalted butter
4 large eggs
¼ cup (50 ml) whipping cream
¼ cup (50 ml) coconut flour
½ tsp vanilla powder or 1 tsp pure
    vanilla extract
1 tsp baking powder
butter for frying

METHOD:

Whip cream, if serving.

    Melt butter. Beat eggs until foamy. Stir in whipping cream and melted, cooled butter into the egg mixture. If using vanilla extract, add it now.

    Combine coconut flour, vanilla powder—if using— and baking powder. Stir into the batter, making sure there are no lumps. Let rest at least 5 minutes.

    These pancakes are best cooked on barely medium heat, and in a cast iron skillet. You'll soon get the feel for when the pancake is firm enough to flip. Watch carefully so it doesn't burn. Serve pancakes with lightly whipped cream and fresh berries.

Waffles

SERVES 10

Ingredients:

1½ tbsp (25 g) unsalted butter

5 large eggs

3 tbsp erythritol powder and ¹⁄₁₆ tsp
    stevia powder

1 cup (200 ml) whipping cream

1 cup (200 ml) crème fraîche

½ cup (100 ml) coconut flour

1 tsp baking powder

½ tsp vanilla powder or 1 tsp pure
    vanilla extract

METHOD:

Melt butter. Whip cream, if serving.

Beat eggs and sweetener until light and airy. Whisk in whipping cream and crème fraîche, then pour in the butter. If using vanilla extract, add it now.

Combine coconut flour with baking powder and—if using—vanilla powder. Mix thoroughly into batter, making sure there are no lumps. Let rest at least 5 minutes.

Use a well heated waffle iron but expect these waffles to need a little bit more time than traditional wheat waffles. Serve the freshly baked waffles with whipped cream and fresh berries.

◆➤ **TIP:** Leave batter on the waffle iron for just under half a minute before lowering the lid. The waffles will be somewhat thicker, and will be easier to remove.

USEFUL LINKS:

For more recipes and updates, visit me at my blog, Mariann's LCHF:
www.mariannslchf.com

Information about LCHF:
www.dietdoctor.com
www.eatingacademy.com
www.drbriffa.com
www.wheatbellyblog.com
www.diabetes-book.com
www.proteinpower.com/drmike
www.carbsmart.com

Low-Carbohydrate and LCHF forum:
http://www.lowcarbfriends.com/bbs/

Online Merchants for LCHF products:
www.iherb.com
www.netrition.com
www.vitacost.com
www.nutrafiber.com

Check out your local food co-ops and health food stores for LCHF staples such as coconut and almond flour, erythritol, and stevia. (Psyllium husk can often be found among the ever-growing selection of gluten-free products in well-stocked supermarkets.) If they don't have what you're looking for, ask for it. Feel free to inquire about those items at your regular grocery store as well, because the higher the demand, the sooner and wider the availability of these alternative products at the supermarket.

ACKNOWLEDGMENTS:

There are many people who encouraged me along the way in the writing and publishing of this book, to whom I wish to extend a big and heartfelt thank you for their invaluable contributions: to my friends and family, who tasted my pastries and gave me advice; to those who read through the drafts of the manuscript and assisted me with their expertise and helpful suggestions; to all who contributed their beautiful china, tablecloths, and silverware; and finally to my beloved daughter Elisabeth, whose unwavering support has been both wonderful and immeasurable to the creation of this baking book—it wouldn't have turned out quite as pretty if it hadn't been for you! Thank you!

And a special thank you to my friend Gun Penhoat, who gave me my American voice, and whose knowledge about Swedish and American cooking has been absolutely invaluable in the making of this English edition. She is a highly experienced low carb high fat baker, and I am most grateful for her support and assistance.